AMSTERDAM CASTLE MUIDERSLOT

Waanders Uitgevers, Zwolle
Rijksmuseum Muiderslot, Muiden

Contents

Uniquely itself since 1285

Muiderslot Castle has stood just outside Amsterdam for over 700 years. This ancient castle is a magical place, surrounded by greenery and water. Built by Count Floris V in 1285, during its long history it has been used as a home, besieged and occupied, demolished, rebuilt and refurbished. This book tells the turbulent story of the finest and best-preserved Medieval castle in the Netherlands, now a lively placed enjoyed by many visitors.

The finest and best-preserved Medieval castle in the Netherlands

Defensive stronghold

Muiderslot Castle was built as a defensive stronghold, its walls no less than 1.5 metres thick. Guards would watch over the surrounding area from the towers that protrude above its walls. No enemy could scale the walls unseen, having already been spotted from one of the 48 embrasures as they approached.

A warm welcome

The Gate Tower was the heart of the defences at Muiderslot Castle. It was a kind of control room from which the soldiers were issued with instructions. Immediately above the castle gate was the machicolation, three holes through which boiling oil, pitch, bricks or boiling water would be thrown: a warm welcome for the enemy!

Difficult staircase

To reach the top of the West Tower, the enemy had to climb 83 uneven steps. The narrow winding staircase rotates to the right, and that is no coincidence. It was extremely difficult to climb with a drawn sword in one's right hand, fighting all the way up.

Flying scaffolding

On the large covered walkway and by some windows there were holes in the outer wall, through which one could push a beam, then climb through the window and lay a plank across the beams to make a kind of flying scaffolding that served as an extra line of defence.

Stone cannonballs

Towards the end of the Middle Ages, around 1500, 'round shot' came into use: stone cannonballs with huge destructive force. No castle wall could withstand them. The first volley of cannonballs would loosen the stonework, and the next series to be fired would break right through it. This signalled the end of the castle as a defensive weapon.

A glorious spot

The story of Muiderslot Castle begins in the Middle Ages. Around 1285 Floris V, Count of Holland and Zeeland, had an imposing stronghold built at a strategic location by the mouth of the river Vecht, close to the Zuyder Zee. At that time the Vecht was the most important trading route by water to Utrecht. Floris made every ship that passed pay a toll. That earned him a pretty penny, and it also gave him complete control over who entered and left the bishopric of Utrecht. This was a thorn in the side of his greatest enemy, the bishop of Utrecht, all the more so since Count Floris had also acquired the rights to the bishop's territory.

They fall together

Floris V was a progressive ruler and an ambitious strategist, with useful high-ranking international contacts. The English king Edward I was an ally, for example.

Floris reorganised the County of Holland and stripped the aristocracy of their administrative role. He also raised a number of wealthy farmers to the aristocracy. This made him popular with the people, who nicknamed him 'God of the Farmers'.

As he gained more territory, rights and money, the count made new friends and new enemies.

His successful divide and rule strategy eventually became his downfall. On 23 June 1296 the unsuspecting count was captured while out hunting with friends, and imprisoned in his own Muiderslot Castle!

The people came to Floris' aid and his captors quickly fled, taking the count with them. They encountered his supporters at Muiderberg. Floris was defenceless, as he was tied to a horse. He ended up in a ditch and was brutally murdered by Gerard van Velzen.

Picture from a school textbook showing the capture of Floris, by well-known illustrator J.H. Isings.

'Murder of Count Floris the Fifth' in Jan Wagenaar, *Vaderlandse Historie*, 1720.

The first political murder in the Netherlands

Political murders were common in many countries. The first political murder to occur in the Netherlands was the killing of the popular Count Floris V in 1296. The news spread round Europe like wildfire.

Razed to the ground

Floris V was succeeded by his son John, who at the time was still a minor, training as a knight at the English court. The bishop of Utrecht saw an opportunity, hurried to Muiden, stormed the castle and razed it to the ground. This turned out to be a very clever move: the people were able to vent their anger, and the hundreds of thousands of bricks were taken away up the Vecht for the extension of Vredelant Castle, a little further upriver. This meant that Muiderslot Castle could not be rebuilt quickly, and the bishop regained control over trade in the region and the river.

The bricks from Vredelant Castle were recycled again in the 16th century for Vredenburg Castle in Utrecht.

Count Floris V (1254-1296), son of a king and castle builder

Anonymous illustration of the young Floris, painted in the 15th century.

Double portrait of King William II and his son, Count Floris V, in Hendrik van Heessel's 1415 book of heraldry.

An imprint of Count Floris V's knight's seal. The seal was broken immediately after his death, to ensure it was not misused in his name.

Born the son of a king

Floris V was a small child when his father was murdered by the West Frisians. Little Floris was later taught about a king's son who avenged his murdered father, so he knew from a young age what was expected of him. He officially become Count of Holland at the age of twelve.

Great castle builder

Like his father, Floris V was a powerful monarch. He ruled the region that is now Noord-Holland, Zuid-Holland and Zeeland provinces. In 1282 he defeated his mortal enemies who had murdered his father, the West Frisians. He quickly built five castles at Medemblik, Alkmaar and Wijdenes to form a ring of defences around his entire territory. All five were built in just six years – an amazing feat of construction.

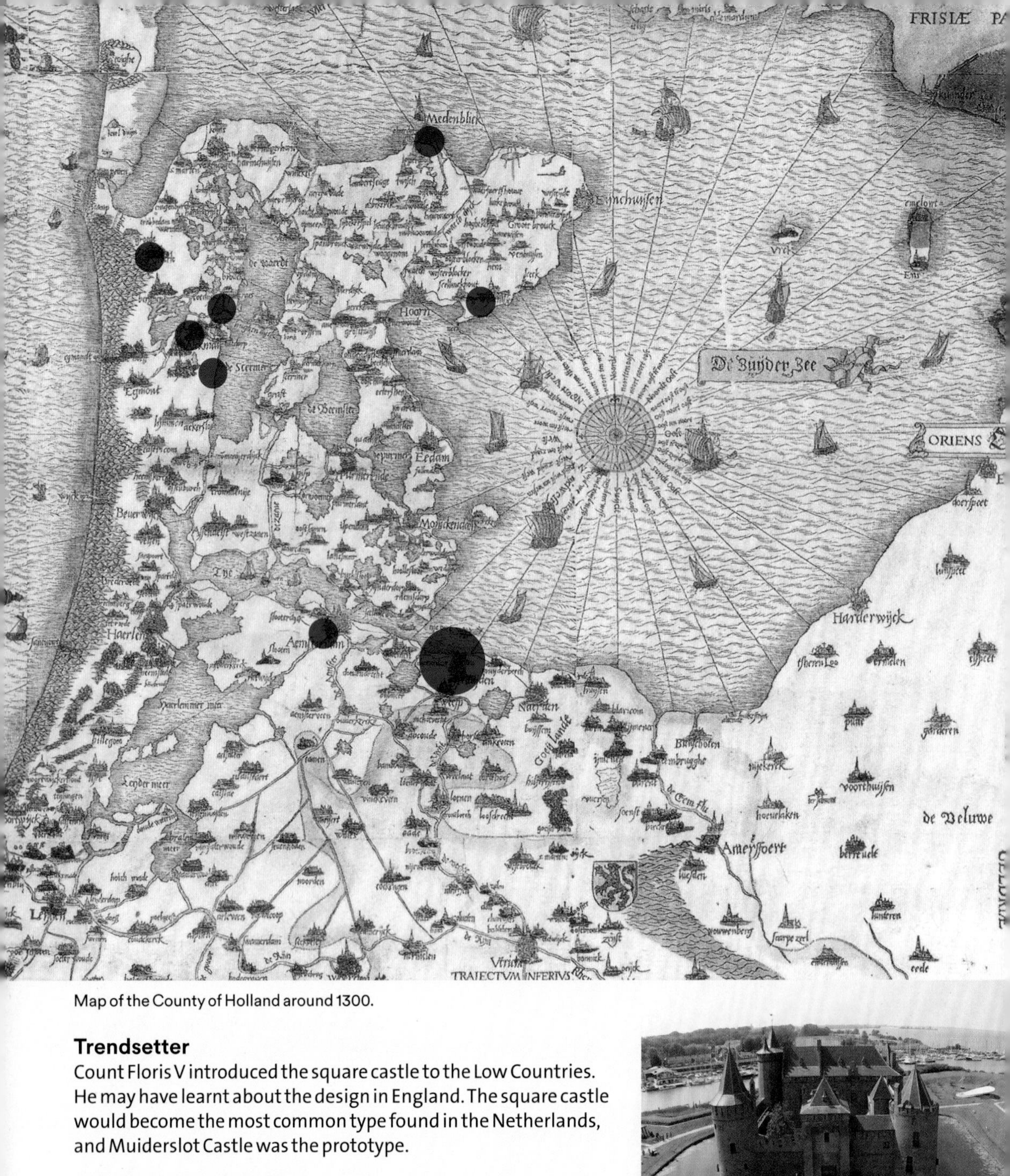

Map of the County of Holland around 1300.

Trendsetter

Count Floris V introduced the square castle to the Low Countries. He may have learnt about the design in England. The square castle would become the most common type found in the Netherlands, and Muiderslot Castle was the prototype.

At home in The Hague

When he was not traveling Floris V lived in The Hague. He was married to Beatrice of Flanders, and together they had seven children, only one of whom, John, survived beyond the age of ten. He is the 'Jantje' whose statue stands beside Hofvijver lake beside the parliament building in The Hague. He points to the 'Binnenhof', the seat of the Dutch government. He also features in the lyrics of a well-known song about The Hague.

In the name of the count

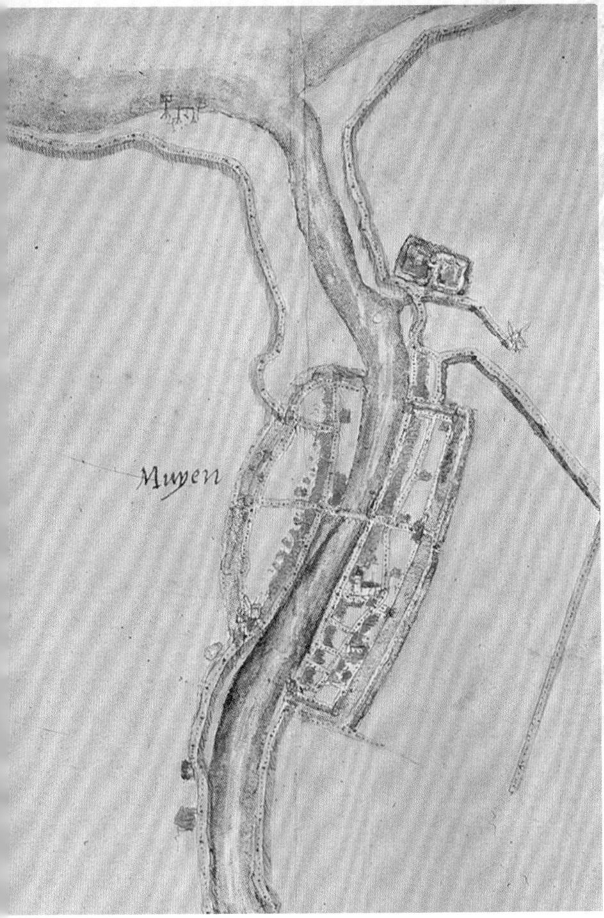

Jacob van Deventer sketched this bird's-eye view of Medieval Muiden and Muiderslot Castle around 1560.

Albert, Duke of Bavaria, who was also Count of Holland, decided to rebuild and even extend the original Muiderslot Castle around 1370, in view of its strategic location relative to Utrecht and Friesland.

Albert himself lived in the Knights' Hall in The Hague, which was also built by Count Floris V. The bailiff of the Gooi region lived at Muiderslot Castle. The bailiff was an important administrator and the count's confidant and representative. The role was introduced by Floris' father. The bailiff would levy tolls, maintain order and, as dike reeve, was also responsible for managing the dikes. He oversaw hunting and beachcombing, and was a judge, with the power to imprison people and conduct trials at the castle.

Count Floris V built the Knights' Hall in The Hague as his home. It was based on Westminster Hall in London.

Mirror punishments

Mirror punishments were imposed in the Middle Ages. The idea was that the punishment should reflect the crime, so a small misdemeanour would be punished by a fine or banishment. The fine might be a sum of money, or the provision of goods or materials that were needed at that moment. If the city walls needed repairing, for example, the offender would be required to provide stones or bricks.

Defensive stronghold

Muiderslot Castle was intended mainly as a defensive stronghold. In times of peace the castellan and his family would live there. When there was a threat of hostilities, and at times of war, soldiers would be stationed at the castle, in the room which is now the armoury.

Identifying colours

The aristocracy used the colours of their family crest at their castles, on flags and on clothing. Knights and soldiers clearly wore the colours on their armour and weaponry. Red was the colour of the House of Holland, and the lion featured in their family crest. One important resident of the castle who knew all about family colours, coats of arms and flags was the herald of arms. He would record his knowledge in a heraldry book. The herald could tell from far away whether a friend or foe was approaching, on the basis of their clothing, coat of arms and the plumes on the helmets. The castle could then prepare a suitable welcome.

The heraldry room in the Gate Tower.

From the Middle Ages the bailiff, castellen of Muiderslot Castle, lived in the East Tower.

Jacoba of Bavaria

The most famous Medieval woman associated with Muiderslot Castle was Jacoba of Bavaria, who inherited the title Countess of Holland in 1417. On paper, everything seemed to be in her favour: she had a high-ranking title, status and many assets. Jacoba was in power during a turbulent period in which the nobility and her own family contested her position. She married four times, but remained childless, and that was her great misfortune. Without an heir, as a woman she did not have the power to turn the political rivalry to her advantage. In 1433 she was forced to relinquish her titles to her cousin, the powerful Philip, Duke of Burgundy.

The Jane (2017) by artist/photographer Isabelle van Zeijl was inspired by strong women of arms like Joan of Arc. However, she believes it is a woman's beauty that is her secret weapon, not her armour!

The power of women in the Middle Ages

Power was the domain of men. Marriage also served political power and the interests of dynasties, as it was used to forge alliances, expand territory or acquire status. The power of women was closely connected to marriage. They could provide heirs, thus maintaining the dynasty.

The inscription inside this Late Medieval ring – 'Je me tien', I shall uphold it – underlines the significance of marriage as a business contract.

Commercial interests

Amsterdam grew, as did the commercial interests of the County of Holland. Goods were transported mainly by ship. The river Vecht gradually declined in importance as a trading route, as the main route for Hanseatic trade by water shifted to Amsterdam in the course of the fourteenth century. It now passed right by Muiderslot Castle, via the Zuyder Zee towards the Baltic. Traffic over land to Amsterdam became more and more important.

The County of Holland around 1570. In the 13th century a lot of marshland was converted to farmland. The draining of the land caused it to subside to below sea level. New dikes provided protection from the water, and were used for transport over land.

A touch of Burgundian grandeur

Under Philip, Holland was part of the Duchy of Burgundy, a territory as large as today's Benelux. The new ruler governed from his court in Dijon, and the new regime did not go unnoticed at Muiderslot Castle. A bailiff (an administrative official) now lived in style at the castle, and the austere interior of the old fortress finally acquired some colour and grandeur. The chapel was fitted with stained glass windows, and beautifully carved heads now decorated the fireplaces in the main residential rooms.

The fireplace decorated with sculpted heads in the cabinet.

Samengesteld ensemble van haardstenen uit de 16e en 17e eeuw.
De bovenste steen - deksteen of cronement genoemd - is versierd met het wapen van Keizer Karel V (1500-1558).
Composition of fireplace stones from the 16th and 17th centuries.
The upper semicircular capstone is decorated with the coat of arms of Emperor Charles V (1500-1558).

Life at a Medieval castle

Few comforts

The thick brick walls of a castle soon became damp. Glazed windows were still a rarity, so the window opening would be closed using shutters, or a pig's bladder would be stretched over it. Little daylight entered the rooms through the embrasures, and there was always a draught.

Round the fire

There is one golden rule in a castle: find the fireplaces, and you will find the occupants. It was difficult to heat an entire room and make it a pleasant place to be, so only a few would be used as living quarters. These rooms had an open hearth, and everyone would get as close to the warmth and light of the fire as possible, where they would tell each other stories before retiring early for the night.

Privacy?

People had very different ideas about privacy in the Middle Ages. There was no distinction between living, working and sleeping accommodation, and people lived, worked and spent the night in any room with a fireplace. People would sleep, wash, go to the toilet, even have sex in the presence of others.

Op je gemakje

The conveniences, or toilets, would generally be in the residential quarters. Conveniences protruded from the castle walls and did not usually have a door. People would therefore do their business in full view of everyone, simply continuing their conversation as they did so, while everything fell into the moat beneath, providing food for the fish. But imagine what happened in winter, when everything was frozen for a long time...

Medieval colour

The Middle Ages were nowhere near as austere and colourless as we think. People were in fact fascinated by colour. The richer a person was, the more colour they would have around them. The Cabinet at Muiderslot Castle served as living accommodation for the women. The word for cabinet in Dutch, kemenade, is taken from the Latin 'camera caminata', which means heated room.

The Cabinet in 2016, temporarily decorated in Medieval colours.

Mighty Amsterdam

In 1508 the Duke of Guelders and his troops were defeated near Muiden. The Duke wanted Muiderslot Castle, which would allow him to take over the city.

Amsterdam evolved into the most powerful city in Holland county, producing large amounts of revenue for the Count. But where there was a lot of power and revenue, enemies would always be lurking. Philip, Duke of Burgundy, paid little attention to the protection of his northern interests. Mighty Amsterdam therefore decided to take care of its own protection. In 1477 the city council managed to take over the administration and occupation of Muiderslot Castle. It became the castle of Amsterdam, protecting the city from invasion by land and by water. The fortress would serve the city well.

Turbulent times

The sixteenth century was dominated by the emerging struggle for liberation in the Low Countries, as the power of the cities and the citizens grew at the expense of the old nobility. The County of Holland would from now on be ruled by a 'vogt', or overlord. The Low Countries united in their fight against Spanish occupation. The Eighty Years War (1568-1648) broke out and Holland became an independent region under the leadership of an elected stadtholder.

Amsterdam Castle Muiderslot

Amsterdam anniversary

Count Floris V was instrumental in the development of Amsterdam as an important city. It was he who ensured that, from 27 October 1275, residents of the hamlet of 'Amstelledamme' would no longer be required to pay a toll. This allowed the small village on the Amstel river to evolve into a powerful centre of trade. Amsterdam still celebrates its anniversary every year on 27 October. And of course there are festivities at Amsterdam Castle Muiderslot too!

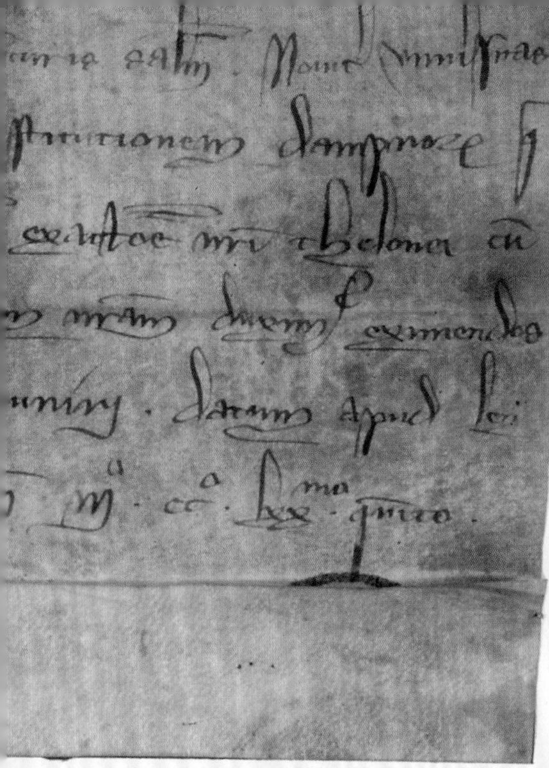

A unique find

During excavations beside the river Amstel on Nieuwedijk in central Amsterdam in 1994, archaeologists found remains of a thick wall beneath the remains of ramparts dating from 1300. Subsequent excavations confirmed the suspicion that the wall belonged to a castle built around 1280: the same time as Muiderslot Castle.

Amsterdam castle

Given the shape of the castle, and political developments and power relationships at that time, the most likely person to have built the castle by the Amstel is Floris V. The count was aware of the importance and potential of the area between the Amstel and the Vecht. To protect and control this area, he began building a new series of fortresses near Amsterdam and Muiden. His untimely death in 1296 meant he was unable to complete the project, however. All castle building came to a halt.

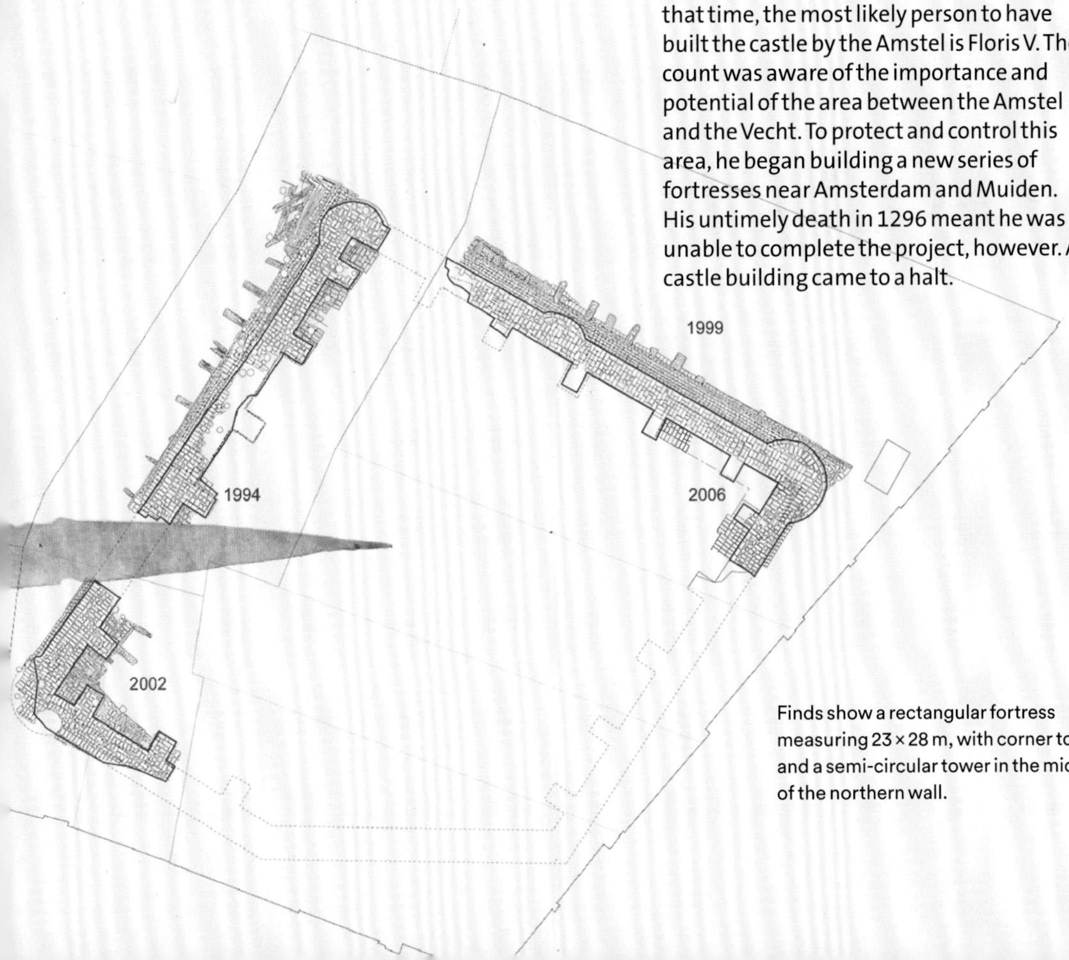

Finds show a rectangular fortress measuring 23 × 28 m, with corner towers and a semi-circular tower in the middle of the northern wall.

Artist in residence

This is believed to be a portrait of Hooft's daughter Christine and her husband Coenraed Burgh posing before Amsterdam Castle Muiderslot. The United East India Company ship 'De Halve Maen' can be seen on the right.

Happier times dawned at Amsterdam Castle Muiderslot in the early seventeenth century with the arrival of author and poet Pieter Corneliszoon Hooft (1581-1647). The son of Amsterdam's mayor, he went to live at Amsterdam Castle Muiderslot when he became the first non-aristocratic burgher in the administration of the Gooi region. He was appointed thanks to the services of his father, Mayor Cornelis Pieterszoon Hooft, who had earned a lot of money working for the United East India Company, and was one Amsterdam's powerful, wealthy administrators.

A home in the Golden Age

Amsterdam Castle Muiderslot was in poor condition when P.C. Hooft moved in. He immediately had maintenance work carried out on the roofs, guttering, walls and windows. The old Medieval fortress was converted into an elegant home, with all the comforts of the Golden Age. Embrasures were made into windows, walls were plastered and a covered vestibule was built onto the knights' hall, where a new fireplace was also installed. The clattering of weapons had been replaced by the sound of poetry, sonnets and songs.

P.C. Hooft taking the oath of office on the bridge in Muiden on 4 June 1609.

A wintry scene at Amsterdam Castle Muiderslot in 1658, painted by J.A. Beerstraten.

Pleasure garden by the Vecht

Amsterdam Castle Muiderslot became a place of pleasure and entertainment outside the city, beside the river Vecht. Hooft had gardens and orchards laid out, and the ramparts were planted with trees to shield his home from the strong winds blowing off the Zuyder Zee. The plums he grew proved particularly enticing to friends and family seeking a pleasant place to stay in the summer.

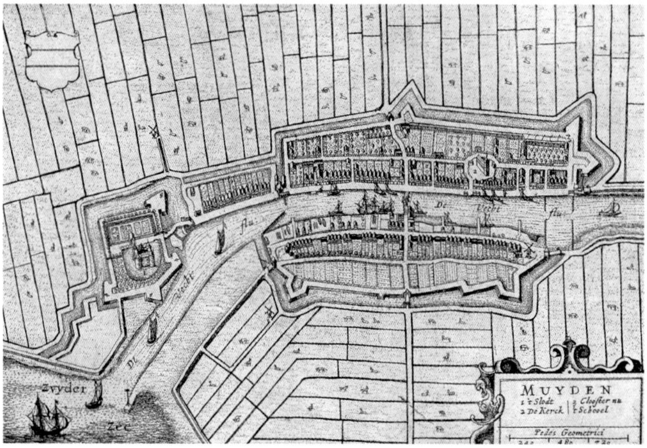

Plan of the fortified town of Muiden and the fortress in a book about towns in Holland county, *Tonneel der steden van Hollandt*, published in 1632.

Home of the Muiden Circle

An eclectic mix of writers, scholars and artists would regularly visit Amsterdam Castle Muiderslot, particularly in summer. Centuries later these leading writers, scientists, administrators, lawyers and artists would come to be regarded as a cultural group, and in the nineteenth century they would enter the history books as the 'Muiden Circle'.

Louis Moritz painted this realistic depiction of the knights' hall with Hooft's famous guests in 1847.

Gerrit Berckheyde painted Amsterdam Castle Muiderslot in the mid- to late 17th century.

Oldest theatre in Amsterdam

P.C. Hooft regularly received members of Amsterdam's theatre world at Amsterdam Castle Muiderslot, where they would perform plays in the knights' hall. Prince Maurits visited in 1619, and the Amsterdam actors performed Hooft's tragedy Isabella specially for him. The knights' hall at Amsterdam Castle Muiderslot is the only remaining theatre that was used by the Amsterdam theatre world in the Golden Age. It is still regularly used as a venue for plays and concerts.

Most famous resident

P.C. Hooft lived at the castle for almost 38 years. He is most famous for his many poems, sonnets, letters and plays, and was an important figure in Dutch literature. The most important literary lifetime achievement award in the Netherlands is still named after him. Hooft was the castle's most famous resident and the main reason why Amsterdam Castle Muiderslot still exists today. He died in 1647, just after paying his respects to the deceased stadtholder Frederick Henry, Prince of Orange

Hooft's study, his 'upstairs office', is on the first floor of the East Tower.

Life in the Golden Age

Princes' Chamber

The Golden Age was a time of prosperity, and this can clearly be seen in the furnished rooms at the castle. The fireplace in the Princes' Chamber bears a gold inscription of P.C. Hooft's motto: 'Omnibus idem', with the sun in the middle. It means 'Everyone is equal'. Hooft intended this in the sense of equal treatment. Just as the sun shines equally on us all, Hooft wanted to see justice done without discrimination.

Family bed

The Hooft family lived in the East Tower. The concept of a bedroom did not yet exist in the seventeenth century, and people would live, work and sleep in any room with a fireplace. People would sleep half seated, as they were scared of losing their minds if they lay down, which they believed would cause too much blood to flow to their head. Children would sleep across the end of the bed.

Fireplace as centrepiece

The fireplace was the centrepiece of every seventeenth-century interior. It was the main source of heat and light in the room. In the summer it would be decorated with garlands of flowers from the gardens. The iron stands on which the firewood lay would often be made of costly materials. The ones in this photograph are made of copper.

Looking at yourself

As well as tapestries, paintings would also adorn the walls of castles. Portraits were particularly popular. Anyone who was anyone would have their portrait hanging on their wall. P.C. Hooft and his wife were immortalised by court painter Michiel van Mierevelt.

Good investment

During receptions, silver and copper objects would gleam on the table and sideboards. They were the ultimate status symbols, and also a good investment, as they could easily be melted down and used as currency in difficult times.

Chairs with a double bottom

The Hooft family and their guests would sit on what were known as 'Spanish' chairs. The cushions – often decorated with the family crest – were much more expensive than the chairs themselves. They also had practical chairs with a storage space under the seat, where they might keep their spectacles, a pipe, money or a bible.

Piles of bills

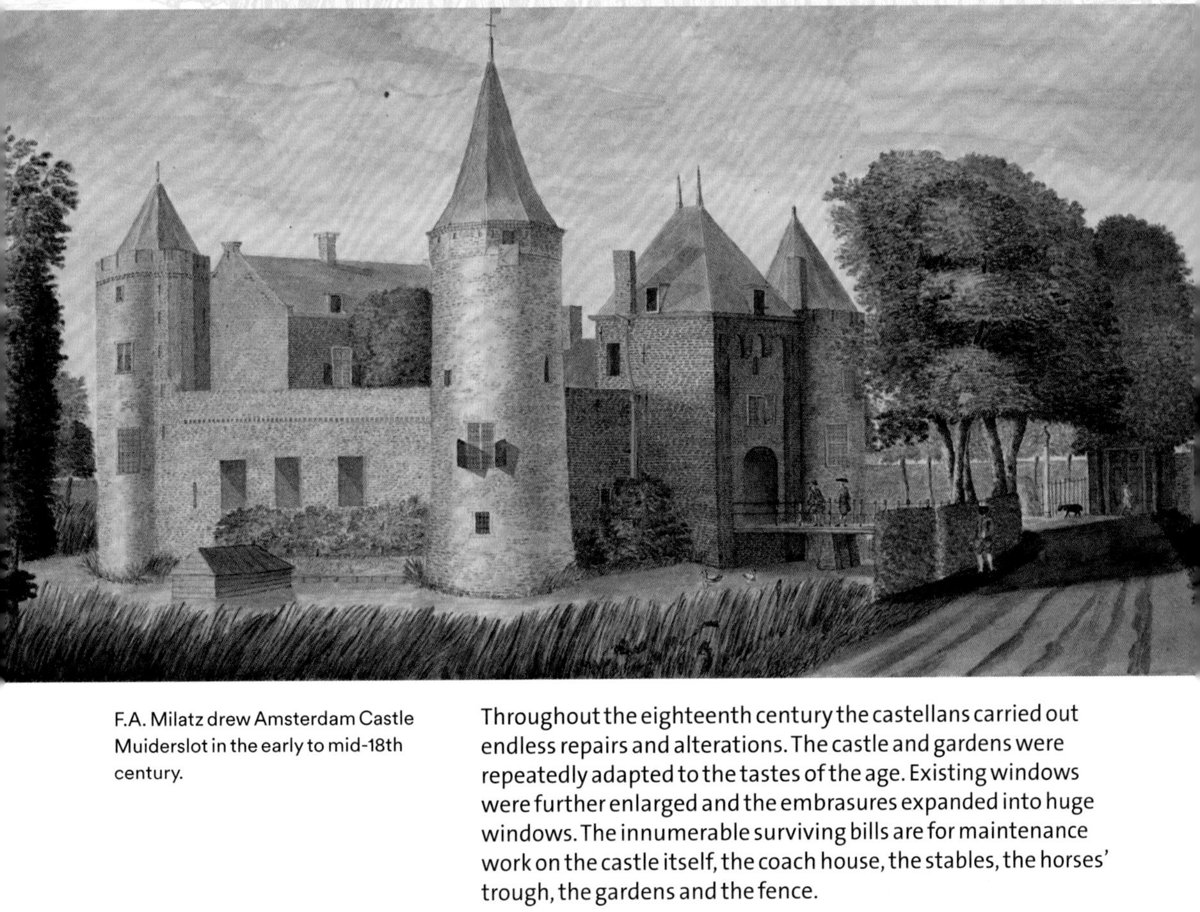

F.A. Milatz drew Amsterdam Castle Muiderslot in the early to mid-18th century.

Throughout the eighteenth century the castellans carried out endless repairs and alterations. The castle and gardens were repeatedly adapted to the tastes of the age. Existing windows were further enlarged and the embrasures expanded into huge windows. The innumerable surviving bills are for maintenance work on the castle itself, the coach house, the stables, the horses' trough, the gardens and the fence.

A dike breach in 1675 between Muiderberg (left) and Amsterdam Castle Muiderslot (right) caused huge damage.

Vulnerable dikes

The ramparts and the wooden dike reinforcements suffered greatly from the saltwater in the Zuyder Zee. To make matters worse, shipworm arrived in the eighteenth century, destroying the underwater wooden piling and weakening the sea dike. A new dike had to be built with stone protection on the seaward side. The damage was so great that eventually all dikes in Holland and Zeeland had to be replaced.

Water as friend and foe

The Counts of Holland were the first to reclaim land from the water. But then they had to protect that land from the water. Centuries later, the water itself was used as a weapon, to flood areas and so prevent the enemy from advancing. The Water Shield Pavilion tells visitors to the castle about the battle against and, above all, *with* the water. The pavilion is located behind the castle. The roof resembles a shield that has been raised slightly, in a reference to Count Floris V's coat of arms.

P. van Loo sketched the castle around 1785.

Castle in decline

The administrative official – the bailiff – who lived at Amsterdam Castle Muiderslot increasingly performed his duties away from home, and rarely stayed at the castle. The castellan was responsible for the day-to-day running of the castle. Panic broke out in 1787 when rebellious patriots advanced from Amsterdam towards Muiden and occupied the castle, which by now belonged to the state, their enemy. The castellan was ejected with force and his priceless porcelain was thrown through the windows into the moat. The castle was plundered and vandalised.

Threat of explosion

Not long afterwards, in 1795, Louis Napoleon of France assumed power in the Low Countries. All civil servants were fired, including the bailiff. French soldiers moved into Amsterdam Castle Muiderslot. On the orders of Napoleon Bonaparte The cellars were packed with weapons and munitions. At one point no less than 90,000 pounds of gunpowder was stored there. The consequences had there been an explosion are unthinkable...

From knight's castle to museum

VOOR HET RYK.

AMORTISATIE SYNDICAAT.

VERKOOPING

VAN

DOMEINEN.

Op Zaturdag den 16den July 1825, des voormiddags ten Elf ure, zal men op het Raadhuis der Stad *Muiden*, ten overstaan van den Heer Burgemeester of deszelfs Gedelegueerde, eerst by opbod, en daarna by afslag, onder nadere hooge approbatie van Zyne Majesteit den KONING, publiek *voor Afbraak*

VERKOOPEN

HET SLOT TE MUIDEN.

Nader onderrigt te bekomen ten Kantore van den Ontvanger der Domeinen te *Weesp*, alsmede by den Opzigter van 's Ryks Fortificatien te *Muiden*. Zullende de Veil-Condities dagelyks ter lezing liggen aan het Kantoor van den bovengemelde Ontvanger; alsmede in het Logement *den Roskam* te *Weesp*, in het *Hof van Holland* te *Muiden*, in de *Kroon* te *Naarden*, te *Amsterdam* in het *Noord-Hollandsche Koffyhuis*, het *'s Gravelandsche Veerhuis* en de *Nieuwe Stads Herberg* aan het *T*, te *Haarlem* in den *Toelast*, te *Alkmaar* in den *Toelast*, te *Utrecht* op het *Vreeburg* in het Logement van *Croes*, te *Gouda* in den *Zalm*, te *Amersfoort* in den *Doelen* en te *Edam* in den *Doelen*. Terwyl het Gebouw door de Gegadigden zal kunnen worden bezigtigd des Dingsdags, Woensdags, Donderdags en Vrydags, waartoe men zich zal moeten vervoegen by den even gemelden Ryks Opzigter, mits niet tusschen twaalf en één uur.

ZEGT HET VOORT.

Notice of the public sale for demolition of the castle at Muiden, 16 July 1825.

For sale, for demolition

The Kingdom of the Netherlands was established after the fall of Napoleon, with King William I as monarch. Amsterdam Castle Muiderslot, once such an imposing structure, had fallen into a state of complete dilapidation and was put up for sale. This prompted a storm of protest, mainly from writers and poets, who thought the castle should be preserved in memory of P.C. Hooft, the 'Shakespeare of Holland', and the castle's most famous resident. The king responded, stepping in to prevent the sale. But the state coffers were empty, and a shocked government tried to sell the castle to Amsterdam. The impoverished city was not interested, however.

Wreck with potential

In the mid-nineteenth century the castle was temporarily smartened up and furnished in 17th-century style for a special event. This made people aware of the potential of Amsterdam Castle Muiderslot as a place of remembrance for P.C. Hooft and the Muiden Circle. The great turnaround for the castle came in 1878, when it officially became a national museum, one of the first in the Netherlands.

Charles Rochussen painted the knights' hall decorated for the Vondel festival on 19 October 1867.

Gerrit Lamberts drew part of the abandoned knights' hall in 1838.

Architect P.J.H. Cuypers' 1880 design for the refurbishment of the Great Hall of Amsterdam Castle Muiderslot.

Pierre Cuypers and the knights' hall

In the late nineteenth century Pierre Cuypers was commissioned to produce a plan for the refurbishment of the knights' hall at Amsterdam Castle Muiderslot in the style of the Golden Age. He was famous for designing Amsterdam's Central Station and Rijksmuseum. Several Amsterdam city festivals were held to raise the initial funds. The festival committee was keen, and kept going to raise funds for the restoration of the interior of Amsterdam Castle Muiderslot. It remains in existence to this day.

Hand-tinted postcard showing the Great Hall as envisaged by Cuypers (1905).

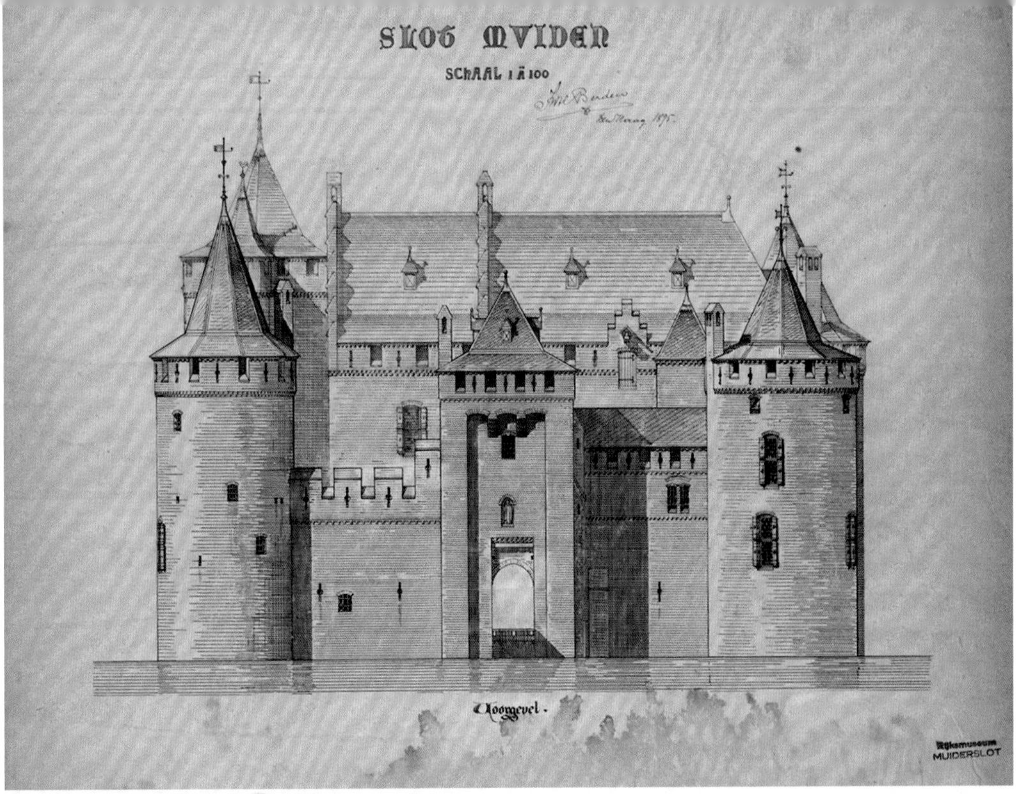

1895 plan for renovation of Amsterdam Castle Muiderslot.

Facelift and battlements

Around 1900 the castle underwent a radical facelift to bring it in line with the romantic image of a Medieval fortress. New battlements were built around the entire castle, plus taller towers with spires and covered walkways. A real functioning well was dug in the inner courtyard. The rickety wooden bridge over the moat was replaced by a stone version.

Generous donors and royal visit

The celebration of the centenary of the kingdom in 1913 was used as an opportunity to organise a major exhibition at Amsterdam Castle Muiderslot. Enthusiasts and museums generously loaned their seventeenth-century furniture, household goods and paintings. Queen Emma was the first to sign the castle's guestbook, followed later by Queen Wilhelmina and her consort. To this day, the guestbook is always signed by high-ranking visitors, such as King Willem-Alexander and Queen Máxima.
In the summer of 1913 40,000 visitors came to the castle, many of them by steam tram from Amsterdam. Some of the objects were donated, purchased or given on long-term loan after the exhibition, so most of the rooms could remain furnished. The interior feels like it did when it was home to P.C. Hooft.

The Princes' Chamber during the 1913 exhibition.

A summer's afternoon with the Muiden Circle

J.H. Isings is the illustrator who created the famous drawings used in Dutch school history textbooks. In 1928 he sketched the Muiden Circle in the knights' hall restored by Cuypers. After the Second World War, during a thorough restoration of the knights' hall, the Medieval fireplace was found. This prompted Isings to adapt his illustration of the Muiden Circle in 1952.

Seven centuries of Muiderslot Castle and water

Through the centuries, Amsterdam Castle Muiderslot evolved from a moated castle to the starting point of the Netherlands' famous water-based defences known as the 'waterlinies'. From the seventeenth century onwards the Dutch developed this unique system of defences which used water as a weapon. When there was a threat of attack, certain areas would deliberately be inundated with a layer of water too deep to walk, ride or drive through, but not deep enough to cross by boat. From 1629 to 1952 Amsterdam Castle Muiderslot was part of no fewer than four waterlinies designed to protect Noord- and Zuid-Holland provinces and Amsterdam: the Utrecht *waterlinie*, the *Oude Hollandse Waterlinie*, the *Nieuwe Hollandse Waterlinie* and the Defence Line of Amsterdam. These lines of defence are world-famous, and are now on UNESCO's World Heritage List.

The 'Sluisbeer' is a hollow stone dam with three lock gates in the outer moat along the bulwark.

Museum inside and out

Once the *Hollandse Waterlinie* was abandoned in the early 1950s, the defences around the castle were no longer protected military terrain. The guard's house in front of the castle made way for reconstructed gardens. In the late 1960s the new gatehouse at the entrance to the site was finished. The last castellan and his family vacated the rooms in the towers, bringing to an end six hundred years of Amsterdam Castle Muiderslot as a home.

This aerial photograph from 1959 shows the herb garden and plum orchard being laid out behind the castle. The ramparts were replanted with elm.

Former living room and bedroom of the castellan, in the North and East Towers respectively.

Amsterdam Castle Muiderslot as highlight

The development and reconstruction of the surrounding site increasingly put the castle in the spotlight. Interest in Floris V and Medieval chivalry also grew. Visitors wanted more than just a guided tour of the house as it would have been in Hooft's day. Amsterdam Castle Muiderslot is the highlight of the collection. Around the turn of the millennium it was thoroughly renovated, and the vast majority of it is now open to the public.

Popular television series like 'Floris' (1960) and 'Game of Thrones' feed the ongoing interest in the age of chivalry.

Falconry

In contrast to ordinary hunting, falconry was a great event for the wealthy in the Middle Ages. It was the preserve of the aristocracy, and Floris V was a great fan. A person's status determined what bird he would use for hunting: an eagle for the emperor, a gyrfalcon for a king and queen, and a peregrine falcon or hawk for the nobility. As the smallest bird of prey, the merlin was popular among noblewomen.

Tour of ramparts and gardens

Simon de Vlieger painted Amsterdam Castle Muiderslot, hidden behind the heavy vegetation on the ramparts, in 1650.

Defensive planting

Trees such as elm, walnut and white poplar were planted on the ramparts as windbreaks. Tall trees such as alder, oak, ash and willow provided timber. Thick vegetation kept invaders out. Trees with abundant foliage like elm, oak and walnut masked the fortress.

Detail from a map in a 1632 book on towns in Holland County, *Tonneel der steden van Hollandt*, showing the castle and gardens

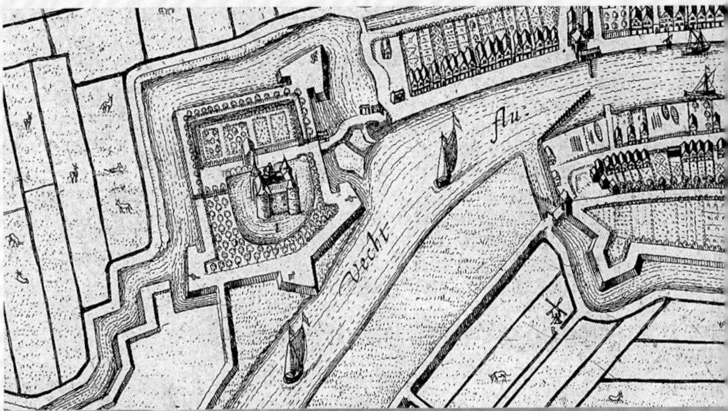

The plum orchard is also back, with no fewer than 18 historic varieties of plum.

P.C. Hooft's gardens

Around 1620 P.C. Hooft had classic ornamental and kitchen gardens and orchards laid out, both for enjoyment and to provide food. A beautiful garden enhanced the owner's status. Hooft therefore opted for a kitchen garden with an ornamental garden, a common combination on country estates in Holland at that time. Hooft's gardens have been reconstructed in the Dutch classicist style, with rectangular forms and pure symmetry. They were restored to their former glory over 60 years ago, and visitors can now enjoy the vegetables (some of them forgotten), herbs, plants, fruit and flowers there. The gardens are expertly cared for by a large group of volunteers. They are happy to talk about the gardens and share seventeenth-century gardening tips.

The herb garden is divided into herbs used for decoration, dyes, medicines and cooking. Time flies as one sits on the circular bench beneath the triple layers of the lime tree.

Shade for the nobility

The gardens are divided and linked by an arcade, a covered walkway formed by trees, with openings that afford magnificent views of the herb, flower and vegetable gardens. The arcade and the layered lime tree in the herb garden provide shade, a privilege that in the past distinguished the pale-skinned nobility from the workers with their weathered skin.

Amsterdam Castle Muiderslot's kitchen garden is the first reconstruction of a Renaissance vegetable garden in the Netherlands.

Timeline

9th century
earliest mention of Amuthon (Muiden).

953
first mention of toll rights at Villa Amuda.

1170
All Saints' Flood: Amuda moves?

1275
Count Floris V grants Amsterdam toll privileges .

1281
Bishop of Utrecht mortgages towns of Muiden and Weesp to Count Floris V.

1281
Count Floris V acquires rights to Muiden and Weesp.

C. 1285
First Muiderslot Castle: four towers linked by walls.

1296
Capture, abduction and murder of Count Floris V.

1297
Muiderslot Castle besieged and razed to ground.

from 1370
Albert, Duke of Bavaria rebuilds Muiderslot Castle.

1386
Small new NE residential wing with chapel.

1428
Treaty of Delft: Jacoba, Duchess of Bavaria loses County of Holland.

1433
Philip III, Duke of Burgundy becomes Count of Holland.

from 1443
A touch of Burgundian grandeur.

C. 1450
Thatched roofs replaced by slate.

1462
Charles the Bold, Duke of Burgundy visits Muiderslot Castle.

1471
New top on South Tower.

1477
Muiderslot Castle becomes Amsterdam Castle Muiderslot

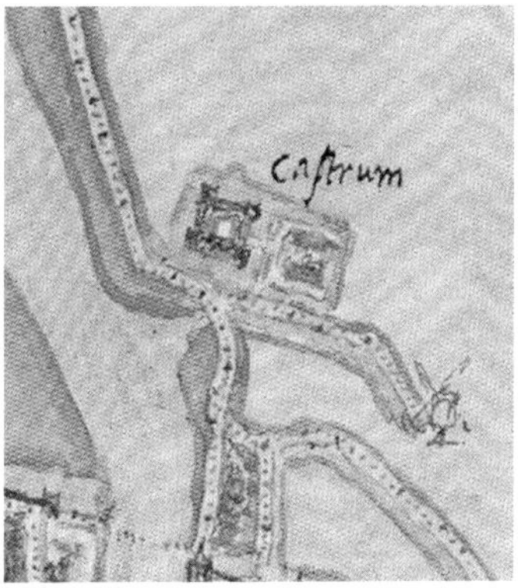

1508-1509
Castle seized and appropriated by Charles, Duke of Guelders.

1576
Amsterdam Castle Muiderslot occupied by Spanish.

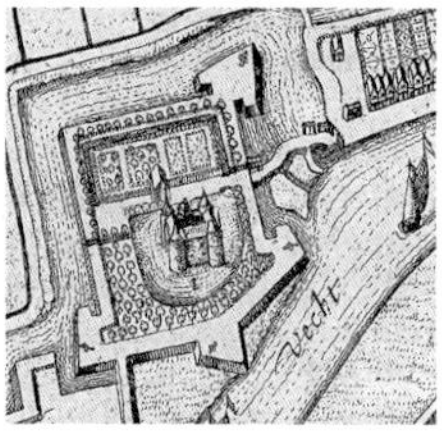

1577
New fortifications built round Amsterdam Castle Muiderslot.

1581
King Philip II last Count of Holland and Zeeland.

1587
English Earl of Leycester occupies Amsterdam Castle Muiderslot.

1609
P.C. Hooft appointed drost (sheriff), bailiff and castellan of Amsterdam Castle Muiderslot.

1618
Play performed for Prince of Orange in knights' hall.

from 1623
More comfort: embrasures made into windows.

1630-1631
Covered gallery added in castle courtyard.

1647
P.C. Hooft dies.

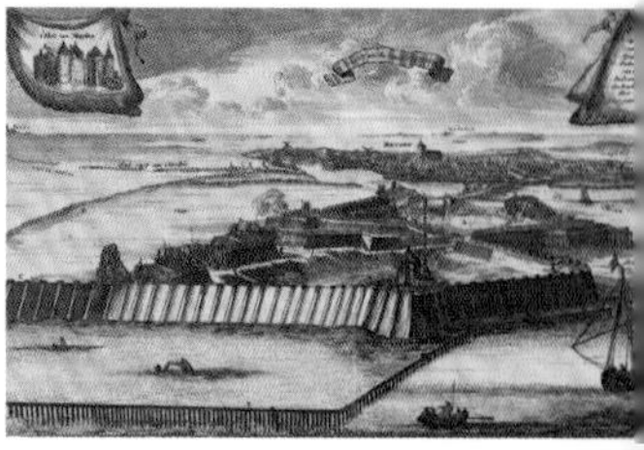

1672
Amsterdam Castle Muiderslot used in defences against French.

1691
First of three new generations of Hooft family bailiff at Amsterdam Castle Muiderslot.

1787
Castle plundered by patriots.

1825
Amsterdam Castle Muiderslot for sale for demolition.

1851
Construction of hollow stone dam, or 'Sluisbeer', part of Waterlinie.

1711-1724
Embrasures in long covered walkway made into picture windows.

1795-1813
Castle in decline under French Napoleonic rule.

1830
Amsterdam Castle Muiderslot becomes property of state.

1815
Amsterdam Castle Muiderslot becomes part of Nieuwe Hollandse Waterlinie.

from 1732
Wooden dike reinforcements replaced by stone.

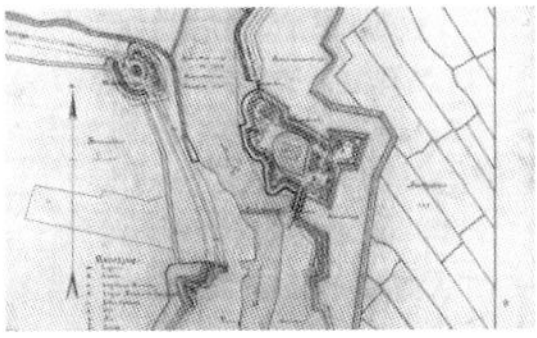

1793-1795
Amsterdam Castle Muiderslot is French barracks and state prison.

1831
First survey as state property.

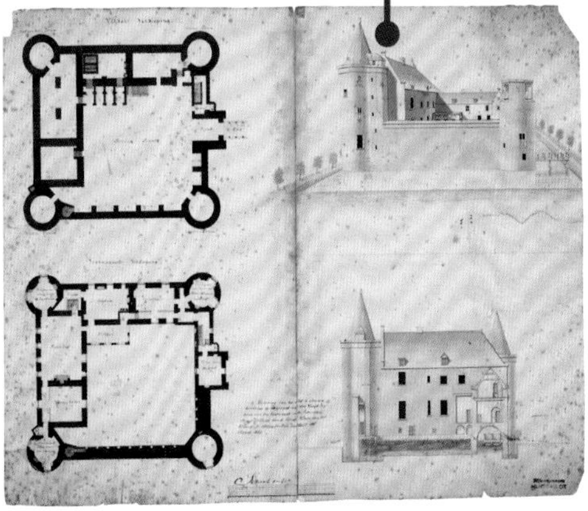

1858-1860
Painter Johannes Hilverdink of Muiden lives and works at the castle.

1867
National Vondel commemoration at Amsterdam Castle Muiderslot.

1876
First photograph of Amsterdam Castle Muiderslot.

1878
Amsterdam Castle Muiderslot becomes state-owned museum.

1881
National celebrations of 300th anniversary of birth of P.C. Hooft. Amsterdam daytrippers visit Amsterdam Castle Muiderslot by Gooi steam tram.
Restoration plans for knights' hall by architect P.J.H. Cuypers.

1895-1909
First major interior and exterior restoration of Amsterdam Castle Muiderslot. Demolition and reconstruction of gallery and well in courtyard.

1913
First major exhibition at Amsterdam Castle Muiderslot.
Queen Emma first person to sign guestbook.

1918
Guard's home built opposite castle; part of military fort.

1939
School at Amsterdam Castle Muiderslot during mobilisation.

1947
Second major Hooft commemoration, refurbishment of museum begins.

1951
First P.C. Hooft Prize (state prize for literature) awarded at Amsterdam Castle Muiderslot.

1969
Completion of gatehouse home for castellan.

1984
Renovation of herb garden.

1981
Celebration of 400th anniversary of birth of P.C. Hooft with bronze plaque in courtyard.

1955
Demolition of stone depots in ramparts.

1952
Castle site transferred to Ministry of War.

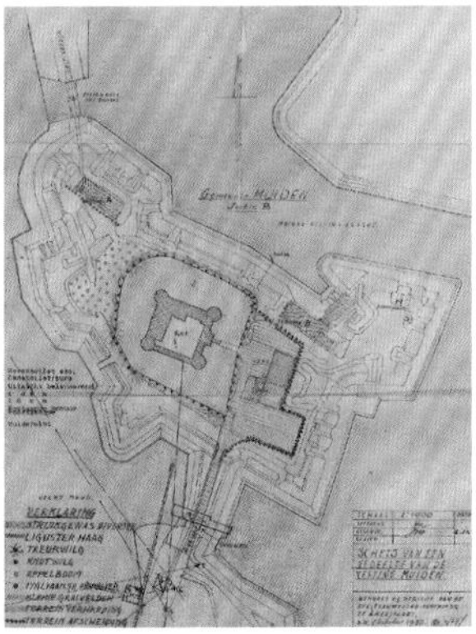

1956-1962
Second major interior restoration of Amsterdam Castle Muiderslot. Chapel opened to public.

1989
Refurbishment of armoury.

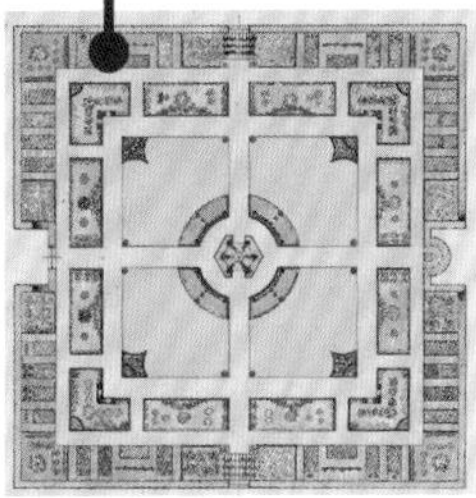

1956
Reconstruction of herb garden in former outer bailey. Planting on reconstructed ramparts.

1995
Amsterdam Castle Muiderslot becomes independent museum.

1996
Commemoration of 700th anniversary of death of Count Floris V.

1999
Kitchen garden laid out in form of Renaissance vegetable garden.

2003
125 years of Amsterdam Castle Muiderslot Museum: Muiden Circle returns to knights' hall.

2004-2006
Plum orchard uprooted and replanted with 17th-century varieties.

2004-2005
Renovation of gatehouse and construction of new entrance and ticket office.

2005-2006
Third major interior renovation and refurbishment of Amsterdam Castle Muiderslot.

2006
Large portion of castle opened to public. Refurbishment of armoury.

2012
Completion of Water Shield in plum orchard.

2015
First 'Hooftjuweel', Amsterdam Castle Muiderslot junior prize for poetry, awarded to Irshaad Kaijoem.

2018
Box hedges in herb garden replaced by boards.

Credits

Publisher
Waanders Uitgevers, Zwolle
Rijksmuseum Muiderslot, Muiden

Author
Yvonne Molenaar

Advise
Henk Boers

Editing
Ben Reef, Cécile Brvar

Copy-editing
Loes Visch

Translation
Sue McDonnell

Design
Harald Slaterus

Printing and lithography
Wilco Art Books, Amersfoort

ISBN 978 94 6262 2517
NUR 688

This publication is also available in a Dutch edition ISBN 978 94 6262 250 0.

www.waandersdekunst.nl
www.muiderslot.nl

Photo credits
All images and rights belong to Rijksmuseum Muiderslot, except for:

© Bas Meeuws **51** (m), **60**, **71** (2018)
Netherlands Institute for Sound and Vision **55** (u)
© Beemflights **4-5**, **16**
© DeRode3D **64-65** (1285, 1297, 1386, 1450)
Hendrik Conscience Heritage Library, Antwerp **15** (l)
© Flying Focus **6**
Monuments, Historic Buildings and Archaeology Department, Amsterdam City Council **33**
Gooise Meren Municipal Authority **34**
© Godert Kieboom **56-57**
The Hague Historical Museum **17** (r)
© IJsfontein **9**
Royal Dutch Antiquarian Society Collection / Rijksmuseum **15** (l)
Royal Library, Brussels **15** (r), **24**
© Kropot **8**, **18-19**, **40**, **55** (a), **70** (2006)
© Mike Bink Photography **20**, **21**, **25**, **26**, **27**, **28-29**, **31**, **38-39**, **41**, **42**, **43** (a), **44** (u), **46-47**, **62-63**, **69** (1989), **70** (2004-2005), **71** (2012)
© Monique Hellemons **2-3**, **12-13**, **61**
National Gallery, London **36** (a), **66** (1623)
© Noord-Holland Provincial Archives **16**
Cultural Heritage Agency of the Netherlands **67** (1831)
Rijksmuseum **14**, **49**
Amsterdam City Archives **32**
Stockholm University Art Collections **58** (u)
© Sandra Buijs **59** (u)
Amsterdam University Library **17** (l), **65** (1477)
© Wolter Noordhoff Publishing **52**